Wilson Fluency® / Basic

Reader Three

Closed Syllables (Multisyllabic Words)

FIRST EDITION

WILSON LANGUAGE TRAINING CORPORATION

www.wilsonlanguage.com

Wilson Fluency® / Basic • Reader 3

Item # WFBR3

ISBN 978-1-56778-318-6
FIRST EDITION

PUBLISHED BY:

Wilson Language Training Corporation
47 Old Webster Road
Oxford, MA 01540
United States of America

(800) 899-8454

www.wilsonlanguage.com

Printed in the U.S.A.

November 2013

Wilson Fluency® / Basic · Reader 3

Chart your progress from drill to drill!

Mark your scores at top of each chart.

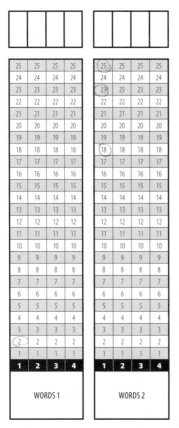

	WORDS 1	WORDS 2	PHRASES 1	PHRASES 2	BASELINE	PHRASED READING	UN-PHRASED READING
Columns	1 2 3 4	1 2 3 4	1 2 3 4	1 2 3 4	1	1 2	1 2

cotton	finish	happen	limit	nutshell
shelf	socks	quick	shop	cloth
fuzz	strands	puff	pick	happen
dress	web	until	rapid	think
cotton	split	things	plant	task

WORDS 2

before	there	people	your	how
Mr.	have	out	could	called
each	into	about	come	would
years	new	were	from	only
first	now	many	you	they

the cotton puff	finish the job
a rapid task	this would limit
had to happen	strands of cotton
until a man	would be split
pick the cotton	in a nutshell
into the cloth	from a cotton plant
people do things	do the job
of the plant	web of thin cotton

about how cotton was made   each seed of the plant

were made into yarn   make this a more rapid task

a man called Mr. Whitney   see if they are made

machine that could do the job   shelf in your bedroom

get cotton cloth more quickly   that helps people do things

Cotton

I bet you have many tops and pants on a shelf in your bedroom. Check out the tags to see if they are made from cotton. Lots of things come from cotton. Did you ever stop to think about how cotton was made?

Before the soft cotton cloth was made into a dress or pants, it was just a puff of a cotton strand. This fuzz or web of thin cotton comes from a cotton plant.

Before the 1790's, people would pick the cotton and then each seed of the plant would be split from the cotton puff. This was the first thing that had to happen. Next, the strands of cotton were made into yarn which was then made into the cloth.

Back then, the seeds were split from the cotton plant by hand. This would limit how much people could finish. For years, this was a big job until a man called Mr. Whitney came along. Mr. Whitney had a plan to make this a more rapid task. He did just that with a new machine that could do the job.

In a nutshell, that is how Mr. Whitney helped people finish the job to get cotton cloth more quickly. Now this is not the only machine that helps people do things more quickly. Now, many things are made by machine and not by hand.

Cotton

I bet you have many tops and pants on a shelf in your bedroom. Check out the tags to see if they are made from cotton. Lots of things come from cotton. Did you ever stop to think about how cotton was made?

Before the soft cotton cloth was made into a dress or pants, it was just a puff of a cotton strand. This fuzz or web of thin cotton comes from a cotton plant.

Before the 1790's, people would pick the cotton and then each seed of the plant would be split from the cotton puff. This was the first thing that had to happen. Next, the strands of cotton were made into yarn which was then made into the cloth.

Back then, the seeds were split from the cotton plant by hand. This would limit how much people could finish. For years, this was a big job until a man called Mr. Whitney came along. Mr. Whitney had a plan to make this a more rapid task. He did just that with a new machine that could do the job.

In a nutshell, that is how Mr. Whitney helped people finish the job to get cotton cloth more quickly. Now this is not the only machine that helps people do things more quickly. Now, many things are made by machine and not by hand.

Chart your progress from drill to drill!

Mark your scores at top of each chart.

The Chicago Fire of 1871 (3.2)

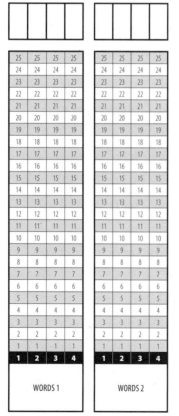

| | WORDS 1 | | | | WORDS 2 | | | | PHRASES 1 | | | | PHRASES 2 | | | | BASELINE | PHRASED READING | | UN-PHRASED READING | |

The Chicago Fire of 1871

swept	visit	Patrick	rustic	frantic
wind	habit	drastic	hectic	happen
travel	problem	fallen	panic	drench
hundred	rest	fall	wild	things
yell	jump	strong	long	flash

WORDS 2

also	called	before	Mrs.	were
down	they	because	water	now
very	people	could	out	been
put	their	your	who	Mr.
over	his	there	years	many

The Chicago Fire of 1871

had a habit

in a panic

went to visit

he sat down

was very drastic

had been hectic

a strong wind

had fallen in

over the land

quick as a flash

and very wild

of their things

a hundred years

the problem was

because the rustic

many people lost all

The Chicago Fire of 1871

jumped over the water

swept up the fire

and Mrs. O'Leary got up

old barn was lit up

all of Chicago was lit up

that no rain had fallen

down to drench out the fire

habit of visiting friends

more than a hundred years ago

is a big city again

The Chicago Fire of 1871

There was a man in Chicago called "Peg Leg" Sullivan who had a habit of visiting friends. In 1871, in the fall, "Peg Leg" went to visit Patrick and Mrs. O'Leary but they were in bed. He sat down to rest, but then in a flash, he got up to yell. In the back of Mr. and Mrs. O'Leary's dwelling, the old barn was lit up. He was in a panic because the rustic shed was on fire. He was frantic.

With his yell, Mr. and Mrs. O'Leary got up, but they could not put the fire out. The problem was that no rain had fallen in a long, long time and now there was a strong wind. Quick as a flash, the fire traveled over the land. The wind swept up the fire and it jumped over the water.

Before long, all of Chicago was lit up. It was very drastic and people could not do much to stop it. At last, rain fell down to drench out the fire. It had been hectic and very wild. So many people lost all of their things. In fact, in the end, much of Chicago was lost.

That happened more than a hundred years ago. Now Chicago is a big city again.

The Chicago Fire of 1871

There was a man in Chicago called "Peg Leg" Sullivan who had a habit of visiting friends. In 1871, in the fall, "Peg Leg" went to visit Patrick and Mrs. O'Leary but they were in bed. He sat down to rest, but then in a flash, he got up to yell. In the back of Mr. and Mrs. O'Leary's dwelling, the old barn was lit up. He was in a panic because the rustic shed was on fire. He was frantic.

With his yell, Mr. and Mrs. O'Leary got up, but they could not put the fire out. The problem was that no rain had fallen in a long, long time and now there was a strong wind. Quick as a flash, the fire traveled over the land. The wind swept up the fire and it jumped over the water.

Before long, all of Chicago was lit up. It was very drastic and people could not do much to stop it. At last, rain fell down to drench out the fire. It had been hectic and very wild. So many people lost all of their things. In fact, in the end, much of Chicago was lost.

That happened more than a hundred years ago. Now Chicago is a big city again.

Chart your progress from drill to drill!

Mark your scores at top of each chart.

Elizabeth Blackwell (3.3)

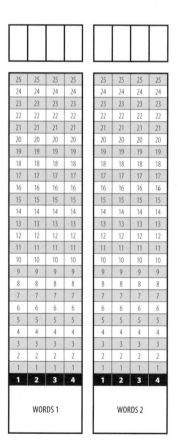

WORDS 1	WORDS 2	PHRASES 1	PHRASES 2	BASELINE	PHRASED READING	UN-PHRASED READING

contract	exact	impact	expect	Blackwell
London	eleven	insist	talent	exist
travel	hundreds	children	well	object
subject	clinic	expand	fact	help
expand	which	class	just	think

WORDS 2

many	people	about	who	should
years	first	could	were	very
one	other	also	people	she
some	into	because	after	they
there	her	be	now	have

could not get

a big impact

just a child

children who were sick

did not think

have much cash

Miss Blackwell also

at the clinic

some people did object

went to London

to help people

there are many

very first one

because they did

years went by

hundreds and hundreds

Elizabeth Blackwell

woman could be a doctor

could get into medical school

a contract for a job

to help others study subjects

was just eleven years old

classes to help other women

she had a big impact

which she should be remembered

the exact number of people

and helped hundreds and hundreds

STORY 3

Elizabeth Blackwell

Who was Elizabeth Blackwell? Many people do not know about her, but Miss Blackwell was very talented and she had a big impact for which she should be remembered.

In 1832, Elizabeth traveled to America when she was just a child. In fact, she was just eleven years old. She did well with subjects at school. Many years went by and Miss Blackwell became the first woman doctor in America. Some people did object because they did not think that a woman could be a doctor. At first, she could not get a contract for a job. Then she started a clinic to help people who did not have much cash. She insisted that they could get help. Miss Blackwell did just that for many, many women and children who were sick. She expanded the clinic and helped hundreds and hundreds of other ill people. In fact, her clinic existed for 90 years. They do not have the exact number of people who were helped.

At the clinic, Miss Blackwell also held classes to help other women so that they could get into medical school. She went to London to help others study subjects to be doctors. Now there are many woman doctors in America. Miss Blackwell should be kept in mind as the very first one.

Elizabeth Blackwell

Who was Elizabeth Blackwell? Many people do not
know about her, but Miss Blackwell was very talented
and she had a big impact for which she should be
remembered.

In 1832, Elizabeth traveled to America when she was
just a child. In fact, she was just eleven years old. She did
well with subjects at school. Many years went by and Miss
Blackwell became the first woman doctor in America.
Some people did object because they did not think that
a woman could be a doctor. At first, she could not get
a contract for a job. Then she started a clinic to help

people who did not have much cash. She insisted that they could get help. Miss Blackwell did just that for many, many women and children who were sick. She expanded the clinic and helped hundreds and hundreds of other ill people. In fact, her clinic existed for 90 years. They do not have the exact number of people who were helped.

At the clinic, Miss Blackwell also held classes to help other women so that they could get into medical school. She went to London to help others study subjects to be doctors. Now there are many woman doctors in America. Miss Blackwell should be kept in mind as the very first one.

Chart your progress from drill to drill!

Mark your scores at top of each chart.

WORDS 1 – 1	WORDS 1 – 2	WORDS 1 – 3	WORDS 1 – 4	WORDS 2 – 1	WORDS 2 – 2	WORDS 2 – 3	WORDS 2 – 4
25	25	25	25	25	25	25	25
24	24	24	24	24	24	24	24
23	23	23	23	23	23	23	23
22	22	22	22	22	22	22	22
21	21	21	21	21	21	21	21
20	20	20	20	20	20	20	20
19	19	19	19	19	19	19	19
18	18	18	18	18	18	18	18
17	17	17	17	17	17	17	17
16	16	16	16	16	16	16	16
15	15	15	15	15	15	15	15
14	14	14	14	14	14	14	14
13	13	13	13	13	13	13	13
12	12	12	12	12	12	12	12
11	11	11	11	11	11	11	11
10	10	10	10	10	10	10	10
9	9	9	9	9	9	9	9
8	8	8	8	8	8	8	8
7	7	7	7	7	7	7	7
6	6	6	6	6	6	6	6
5	5	5	5	5	5	5	5
4	4	4	4	4	4	4	4
3	3	3	3	3	3	3	3
2	2	2	2	2	2	2	2
1	1	1	1	1	1	1	1

PHRASES 1 – 1	PHRASES 1 – 2	PHRASES 1 – 3	PHRASES 1 – 4	PHRASES 2 – 1	PHRASES 2 – 2	PHRASES 2 – 3	PHRASES 2 – 4
50	50	50	50	50	50	50	50
49	49	49	49	49	49	49	49
48	48	48	48	48	48	48	48
47	47	47	47	47	47	47	47
46	46	46	46	46	46	46	46
45	45	45	45	45	45	45	45
44	44	44	44	44	44	44	44
43	43	43	43	43	43	43	43
42	42	42	42	42	42	42	42
41	41	41	41	41	41	41	41
40	40	40	40	40	40	40	40
39	39	39	39	39	39	39	39
38	38	38	38	38	38	38	38
37	37	37	37	37	37	37	37
36	36	36	36	36	36	36	36
35	35	35	35	35	35	35	35
34	34	34	34	34	34	34	34
33	33	33	33	33	33	33	33
32	32	32	32	32	32	32	32
31	31	31	31	31	31	31	31
30	30	30	30	30	30	30	30
29	29	29	29	29	29	29	29
28	28	28	28	28	28	28	28
27	27	27	27	27	27	27	27
26	26	26	26	26	26	26	26
25	25	25	25	25	25	25	25
24	24	24	24	24	24	24	24
23	23	23	23	23	23	23	23
22	22	22	22	22	22	22	22
21	21	21	21	21	21	21	21
20	20	20	20	20	20	20	20
19	19	19	19	19	19	19	19
18	18	18	18	18	18	18	18
17	17	17	17	17	17	17	17
16	16	16	16	16	16	16	16
15	15	15	15	15	15	15	15
14	14	14	14	14	14	14	14
13	13	13	13	13	13	13	13
12	12	12	12	12	12	12	12
11	11	11	11	11	11	11	11
10	10	10	10	10	10	10	10
9	9	9	9	9	9	9	9
8	8	8	8	8	8	8	8
7	7	7	7	7	7	7	7
6	6	6	6	6	6	6	6
5	5	5	5	5	5	5	5
4	4	4	4	4	4	4	4
3	3	3	3	3	3	3	3
2	2	2	2	2	2	2	2
1	1	1	1	1	1	1	1

BASELINE – 1	PHRASED READING – 1	PHRASED READING – 2	UN-PHRASED READING – 1	UN-PHRASED READING – 2
248	**248**	**248**	**248**	**248**
245	245	245	245	245
240	240	240	240	240
235	235	235	235	235
230	230	230	230	230
225	225	225	225	225
220	220	220	220	220
215	215	215	215	215
210	210	210	210	210
205	205	205	205	205
200	200	200	200	200
195	195	195	195	195
190	190	190	190	190
185	185	185	185	185
180	180	180	180	180
175	175	175	175	175
170	170	170	170	170
165	165	165	165	165
160	160	160	160	160
155	155	155	155	155
150	150	150	150	150
145	145	145	145	145
140	140	140	140	140
135	135	135	135	135
130	130	130	130	130
125	125	125	125	125
120	120	120	120	120
115	115	115	115	115
110	110	110	110	110
105	105	105	105	105
100	100	100	100	100
95	95	95	95	95
90	90	90	90	90
85	85	85	85	85
80	80	80	80	80
75	75	75	75	75
70	70	70	70	70
65	65	65	65	65
60	60	60	60	60
55	55	55	55	55
50	50	50	50	50
45	45	45	45	45
40	40	40	40	40
35	35	35	35	35
30	30	30	30	30
25	25	25	25	25
20	20	20	20	20
15	15	15	15	15
10	10	10	10	10
5	5	5	5	5

Basketball Champs

Atlantis	athletic	Calvin	fantastic	basketball
impress	Bigshot	basket	Manhattan	Wilmington
problems	champs	establish	sandwich	miss
shot	quick	mind	finish	stuck
hands	went	ball	basket	problem

WORDS 2

very	one	would	before	could
was	because	called	people	were
who	into	said	after	day
years	your	put	also	two
about	so	many	do	they

STORY 4

an athletic kid

they called Calvin

in the basket

it would establish

had to finish

a quick sandwich

Atlantis and his dad

before he could

fantastic at basketball

it was because

its last basketball

many math problems

who would be champs

in his hands

on a problem

champs at last

Basketball Champs

for its last basketball game   team had to play Wilmington

then went to the game   get two points to win

did not think that his brother   and his Manhattan team

had the ball in his hands   that they were impressed

could go with his dad   but his big brother Calvin

STORY 4

Basketball Champs

Atlantis Smith was not an athletic kid, but his big brother Calvin was very athletic. Calvin was fantastic at basketball. Atlantis did not mind. In fact, he was glad when people said that they were impressed with his brother and when they called Calvin, Bigshot Smith. This was not because he was a "big shot," it was because he could put the ball in the basket. He did not miss that much.

Atlantis and his dad went to most of Manhattan's basketball games. Calvin's team kept winning. Then one day, the Manhattan team had to play Wilmington for its last basketball game. It would establish who would be champs.

Atlantis had many math problems to do before he could go to the big game. He had to finish them so he could go with his dad. He got stuck on a problem, but with help, he did it. He and his dad had a quick sandwich and then went to the game.

At the end, the Manhattan team had to get two points to win. Bigshot Smith had the ball in his hands and went to the basket. Atlantis did not think that his brother would miss the big shot.

It hit the rim, but it did not go in! Then Calvin got the ball back and sent a pass. The kid who got the ball shot it into the basket to win. Atlantis and his dad were glad. Calvin, and his Manhattan team, were champs at last.

Basketball Champs

Atlantis Smith was not an athletic kid, but his big
brother Calvin was very athletic. Calvin was fantastic at
basketball. Atlantis did not mind. In fact, he was glad when
people said that they were impressed with his brother
and when they called Calvin, Bigshot Smith. This was not
because he was a "big shot," it was because he could put the
ball in the basket. He did not miss that much.

Atlantis and his dad went to most of Manhattan's
basketball games. Calvin's team kept winning. Then one
day, the Manhattan team had to play Wilmington for its
last basketball game. It would establish who would be
champs.

Atlantis had many math problems to do before he could go to the big game. He had to finish them so he could go with his dad. He got stuck on a problem, but with help, he did it. He and his dad had a quick sandwich and then went to the game.

At the end, the Manhattan team had to get two points to win. Bigshot Smith had the ball in his hands and went to the basket. Atlantis did not think that his brother would miss the big shot.

It hit the rim, but it did not go in! Then Calvin got the ball back and sent a pass. The kid who got the ball shot it into the basket to win. Atlantis and his dad were glad. Calvin, and his Manhattan team, were champs at last.

Holiday of Thanks (3.5)

Chart your progress from drill to drill!

Mark your scores at top of each chart.

25	25	25	25
24	24	24	24
23	23	23	23
22	22	22	22
21	21	21	21
20	20	20	20
19	19	19	19
18	18	18	18
17	17	17	17
16	16	16	16
15	15	15	15
14	14	14	14
13	13	13	13
12	12	12	12
11	11	11	11
10	10	10	10
9	9	9	9
8	8	8	8
7	7	7	7
6	6	6	6
5	5	5	5
4	4	4	4
3	3	3	3
2	2	2	2
1	1	1	1
1	**2**	**3**	**4**

WORDS 1

25	25	25	25
24	24	24	24
23	23	23	23
22	22	22	22
21	21	21	21
20	20	20	20
19	19	19	19
18	18	18	18
17	17	17	17
16	16	16	16
15	15	15	15
14	14	14	14
13	13	13	13
12	12	12	12
11	11	11	11
10	10	10	10
9	9	9	9
8	8	8	8
7	7	7	7
6	6	6	6
5	5	5	5
4	4	4	4
3	3	3	3
2	2	2	2
1	1	1	1
1	**2**	**3**	**4**

WORDS 2

50	50	50	50
49	49	49	49
48	48	48	48
47	47	47	47
46	46	46	46
45	45	45	45
44	44	44	44
43	43	43	43
42	42	42	42
41	41	41	41
40	40	40	40
39	39	39	39
38	38	38	38
37	37	37	37
36	36	36	36
35	35	35	35
34	34	34	34
33	33	33	33
32	32	32	32
31	31	31	31
30	30	30	30
29	29	29	29
28	28	28	28
27	27	27	27
26	26	26	26
25	25	25	25
24	24	24	24
23	23	23	23
22	22	22	22
21	21	21	21
20	20	20	20
19	19	19	19
18	18	18	18
17	17	17	17
16	16	16	16
15	15	15	15
14	14	14	14
13	13	13	13
12	12	12	12
11	11	11	11
10	10	10	10
9	9	9	9
8	8	8	8
7	7	7	7
6	6	6	6
5	5	5	5
4	4	4	4
3	3	3	3
2	2	2	2
1	1	1	1
1	**2**	**3**	**4**

PHRASES 1

50	50	50	50
49	49	49	49
48	48	48	48
47	47	47	47
46	46	46	46
45	45	45	45
44	44	44	44
43	43	43	43
42	42	42	42
41	41	41	41
40	40	40	40
39	39	39	39
38	38	38	38
37	37	37	37
36	36	36	36
35	35	35	35
34	34	34	34
33	33	33	33
32	32	32	32
31	31	31	31
30	30	30	30
29	29	29	29
28	28	28	28
27	27	27	27
26	26	26	26
25	25	25	25
24	24	24	24
23	23	23	23
22	22	22	22
21	21	21	21
20	20	20	20
19	19	19	19
18	18	18	18
17	17	17	17
16	16	16	16
15	15	15	15
14	14	14	14
13	13	13	13
12	12	12	12
11	11	11	11
10	10	10	10
9	9	9	9
8	8	8	8
7	7	7	7
6	6	6	6
5	5	5	5
4	4	4	4
3	3	3	3
2	2	2	2
1	1	1	1
1	**2**	**3**	**4**

PHRASES 2

234
230
225
220
215
210
205
200
195
190
185
180
175
170
165
160
155
150
145
140
135
130
125
120
115
110
105
100
95
90
85
80
75
70
65
60
55
50
45
40
35
30
25
20
15
10
5
1

BASELINE

234	**234**
230	230
225	225
220	220
215	215
210	210
205	205
200	200
195	195
190	190
185	185
180	180
175	175
170	170
165	165
160	160
155	155
150	150
145	145
140	140
135	135
130	130
125	125
120	120
115	115
110	110
105	105
100	100
95	95
90	90
85	85
80	80
75	75
70	70
65	65
60	60
55	55
50	50
45	45
40	40
35	35
30	30
25	25
20	20
15	15
10	10
5	5
1	**2**

PHRASED READING

234	**234**
230	230
225	225
220	220
215	215
210	210
205	205
200	200
195	195
190	190
185	185
180	180
175	175
170	170
165	165
160	160
155	155
150	150
145	145
140	140
135	135
130	130
125	125
120	120
115	115
110	110
105	105
100	100
95	95
90	90
85	85
80	80
75	75
70	70
65	65
60	60
55	55
50	50
45	45
40	40
35	35
30	30
25	25
20	20
15	15
10	10
5	5
1	**2**

UN-PHRASED READING

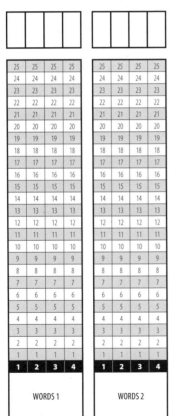

Holiday of Thanks

Pilgrims	travel	landed	prompted	Atlantic
hundred	planted	establish	banquet	fantastic
inhabit	custom	England	recommended	hunted
helping	crops	thanks	ecstatic	extended
giving	wanted	spring	Thanksgiving	things

WORDS 2

how	also	each	about	from
there	new	what	people	have
many	before	now	into	their
two	would	very	they	were
day	years	their	was	look

STORY **5**

the Pilgrims left when they landed

look for land was very cold

recommended many things and many people

they were ecstatic at the banquet

from the Atlantic also had fish

two hundred years their fantastic crops

of giving thanks Thanksgiving is held

extended a helping hand to inhabit the land

land that would become America   plan for the next winter

helped them establish their home   traveled across the Atlantic

not have what they needed   for the help from the Indians

and then President Lincoln wanted   being prompted by Mrs. Hale

a big festival of thanks   at the end of November

Holiday of Thanks

In the fall of 1620, the Pilgrims left England on a ship. They traveled across the Atlantic and when they landed, they were no longer in England. They were on land that would become America. The Pilgrims had to look for land to inhabit, but before long, it was winter. That winter, it was very cold. The Pilgrims did not have what they needed and many people died.

When the cold winter went into spring, the Pilgrims had to think about how to inhabit the land and plan for the next winter. They had help from Indians. The Indians recommended many things to the Pilgrims and extended a helping hand. They hunted and planted their crops with the Pilgrims. They also helped them establish a new home.

In the fall, they had a lot of crops and they were ecstatic. They had a big festival of thanks. At the banquet, they had wild turkey. They also had fish and clams from the Atlantic. This banquet was in thanks for their fantastic crops and for the help from the Indians.

Then, for many years, there was a custom of giving thanks when it was fall. Two hundred years went by and then President Lincoln wanted to establish a day of thanks after being prompted by Mrs. Hale who sent him many letters. Now, in America, Thanksgiving is held at the end of November each year.

Holiday of Thanks

In the fall of 1620, the Pilgrims left England on a ship.

They traveled across the Atlantic and when they landed,

they were no longer in England. They were on land that

would become America. The Pilgrims had to look for

land to inhabit, but before long, it was winter. That

winter, it was very cold. The Pilgrims did not have what

they needed and many people died.

When the cold winter went into spring, the Pilgrims had

to think about how to inhabit the land and plan for the

next winter. They had help from Indians. The Indians

recommended many things to the Pilgrims and extended

a helping hand. They hunted and planted their crops with the Pilgrims. They also helped them establish a new home.

In the fall, they had a lot of crops and they were ecstatic. They had a big festival of thanks. At the banquet, they had wild turkey. They also had fish and clams from the Atlantic. This banquet was in thanks for their fantastic crops and for the help from the Indians.

Then, for many years, there was a custom of giving thanks when it was fall. Two hundred years went by and then President Lincoln wanted to establish a day of thanks after being prompted by Mrs. Hale who sent him many letters. Now, in America, Thanksgiving is held at the end of November each year.

NOTES

NOTES

NOTES

NOTES

NOTES